MAURITIUS FROM ITS ORIGIN

'Au pays parfumé que le soleil caresse...'
'In the perfumed land that the sun caresses...'
Charles Baudelaire

'The more enthusiastic of its inhabitants delight in describing it as the "Pearl of the Ocean". Well, let us call it the "Pearl". It's a good name.'
Joseph Conrad

'...you have stretches of shady dense forest with limpid streams frolicking through them, continually glimpsed and lost and glimpsed again in the pleasantest hide–and–seek fashion; and you have some tiny mountains, some quaint and picturesque groups of toy peaks, and a dainty little vest–pocket Matterhorn; and here and there and now and then a strip of sea with a white ruffle of surf breaks into the view.'
Mark Twain

The author would specially like to thank Dr Jean-Georges Prosper, historian, poet and the author of the Mauritius National Anthem, for correcting the manuscript of this book.

The publisher wishes to thank the Mauritius Government Tourist Office for their kind help and the supply of photographs.
The publisher also thanks Mrs. Nené Weil and Mr. Lorenzo Güller Frers for their generous assistance and for offering their collection of prints and excellent library.

Christian le Comte
PUBLISHER

Published by Christian le Comte
Edited by Mónica Hoss de le Comte

Designed by Christian & Sophie le Comte
Photography on page 64 © Bamba Sourang
Photographies on pages 8 and 10 © MTPA
Christian le Comte, Old Mill Road, Pereybere, Mauritius. Email: books@lecomte.com.ar.
www.christianlecomte.com
Printed in China
ISBN 978-99949-905-1-1

9 789994 990511

MAURITIUS  FROM ITS ORIGIN

by Christian le Comte

Maurits Prins van Oranje.

Preface

The idea for this book was conceived in the year 2000. ¶ It all started when I met, in London, my wife to be & found out that she was from this atoll called Mauritius. Clearly, I had the need to know more about this puzzling place in the heart of the Indian Ocean. ¶ Initial research revealed that a lot of the material about this Dutch, French and British ex-colony was spread all over the world. As my interest grew, a more intensive reading started. ¶ Being in the publishing business, I thought, that there was a lot of unjustifiably forgotten original material, since this small island seemed to have attracted in the last five centuries such diverse and fascinating people. ¶ Soon I found myself overwhelmed by all the stories related to the 'Pearl of the Indian Ocean', which were worth telling. Combining a new and original text with first hand accounts from travellers together with a variety of sources consisting of old prints, historical and modern photography and illustrations, seemed to be hard at first. ¶ However, I thought that the only way to organise all the information, was by telling this story right from the beginning, that is: Mauritius from its origin.

Map of Mauritius.

Contents

The giant bird that Le Guat saw in the island of Rodrigues, 1708.

Aerial view of Mauritius.

Aerial view of the lagoon.

eological Origin

harles Darwin (1809–1882) visited auritius from 29 April to 9 May, 1836.

ap by M. Bonne, 1780 (detail).

n a first inspection of the surface of e Isle of France, there is every reason imagine that it has undergone some olent shock; and that all the stones hich are found on it have been thrown t of a volcano; or that they have oceeded from some general explosion the island.' (Grant)

Mauritius is a 'great mass of volcanic matter' (Darwin) that forms part of a long volcanic chain which stretches from Réunion to the Seychelles.

The first period of volcanic emergence started 10 million years ago. Other periods of volcanic activity and subsequent lava flows followed, forming the three mountain ranges that cross the island: the Port Louis–Moka Mountain Range, the Black River–Savanne Mountain Complex and the Bambous Mountain Massif. The highest mountain is the Piton de la Petite Rivière Noire (828 m) in the southwest.

The central plateau is encircled by the walls of this ancient volcano shield. These inactive volcanoes are higher in the south than in the north, and their summits, as so commonly happens with ancient volcanic rocks, are 'jagged by the sharpest points'.

The coloured earths of Chamarel, are also of volcanic origin. Scientists assert that the uneven cooling of the molten rock formed seven differently coloured layers.

The island of Mauritius is fringed by a broken ring of coral reef, which provides shelter to a beautiful variety of marine life. The stone–like surface of these reefs was formed by calcareous deposits secreted by successive generations of coral polyps. Only the outer surface of the reef is covered by living corals which have found favourable conditions as regards light, constant supply of zooplankton, the necessary content of oxygen, quantities of metallic elements, temperature, winds, ocean currents, etc.

Charles Darwin solved the mystery of the formation of coral reefs when he was reaching Mauritius in April 1836. His explanation is still valid. In his diary on board HMS *Beagle* he writes: 'We see certain islands in the Pacific, such as Tahiti and Eimeo, which are encircled by a coral reef separated from the shore by channels and basins of still water. Various causes tend to check the growth of the most efficient kinds of corals in these situations. Hence if we imagine such an island (figure 1), after long successive intervals to subside a few feet (figure 2), in a manner similar, but with a movement opposite to the continent of South America; the coral would be continued upwards (figure 3), rising from the foundation of the encircling reef. In time the central land would sink beneath the level of the sea and disappear (figure 4), but the coral would have completed its circular wall. Should we not then have a lagoon island? Under this view, we must look at a lagoon island as a monument raised by myriads of tiny architects, to mark the spot where a former land lies buried in the depths of the ocean.'

Figure 1.

Figure 2.

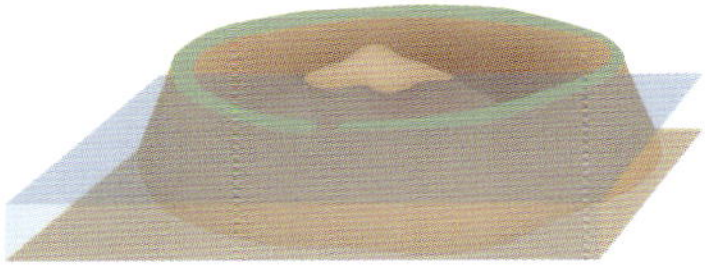

Figure 3.

Figure 4.

Coloured earths of Chamarel.

Early Explorers and New Routes

The history of Mauritius begins at the end of the sixteenth century. Although the island was visited several times by Arab, Portuguese and Dutch people, it remained uninhabited until 1638.

Arab merchants who were trading the in east African coast in the year 1000, sailing the ocean in dhows, not only discovered the Mascarene Islands, but gave the islands a name as well: Rodrigues was called Dina Arabi (deserted island); Mauritius, Dina Mozare (eastern island) and Réunion, Dina Margabim (western island). These traders probably visited the islands, but they never showed any interest in colonising them. Trade is impossible on a deserted island.

Arab merchants.

Ptolomei's World **by Johannes Schnitzer, Ulm, 1482.**

.n the Wake of Vasco da Gama

larco Polo mentions Prester John as he one 'of whose great empire all the world speaks'.

Portuguese vessel.

Vasco da Gama (*c.*1460–1524).

Prince Henry of Portugal called 'the Navigator' (1394–1460) tried to find a way to reach the Indies travelling round the south coast of Africa. He was looking for African gold, the trading route to India and the land of the mythical Christian king, Prester John.

In order to train skilful naval explorers, he created a navigation school in Algarve. The discovery of the route to the East Indies was the result of his school and his quest for the fabulous African king. After Vasco da Gama had successfully rounded the Cape of Good Hope in 1498, other Portuguese expeditions went in his wake and sailed the Indian Ocean.

The islands to the east of Madagascar were given the name of Mascarenhas, after Don Pedro de Mascarenhas, a famous Portuguese captain mentioned in the great Portuguese epic poem *Os Lusiadas*, where the author, Luis de Camões, promises him eternal fame. The Mascarene trio includes Réunion, Mauritius and Rodrigues.

In 1507 Domingo Fernandez Pereira found Mauritius uninhabited and named it 'Ilha do Cerne'.

The origin of this name is not clear, Charles Grant, in his *History of Mauritius*, says 'without doubt' that since Pliny had given the name of Cerna Ethiopia to the Island of Madagascar, Mauritius had to be named Isle of Cerne.

Other historians say that Cerne was the name of Fernandez' ship, and still others that it was called *cerne* (swan), because of the abundance of Dodos.

During the period that comprehended almost the whole of the sixteenth century, the Portuguese made no settlements on any of the Mascarenes and they only occasionally used them to fix damaged ships.

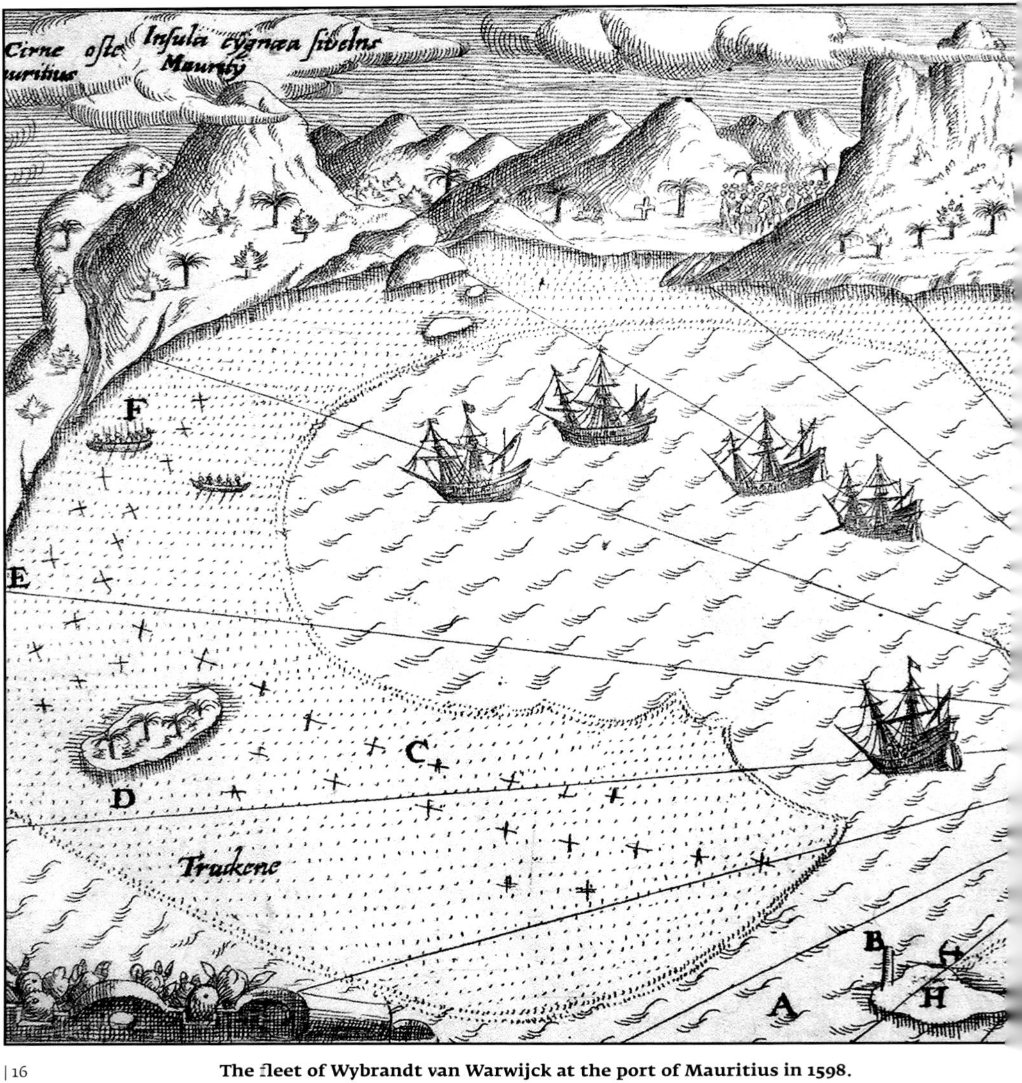

The fleet of Wybrandt van Warwijck at the port of Mauritius in 1598.

he Dutch

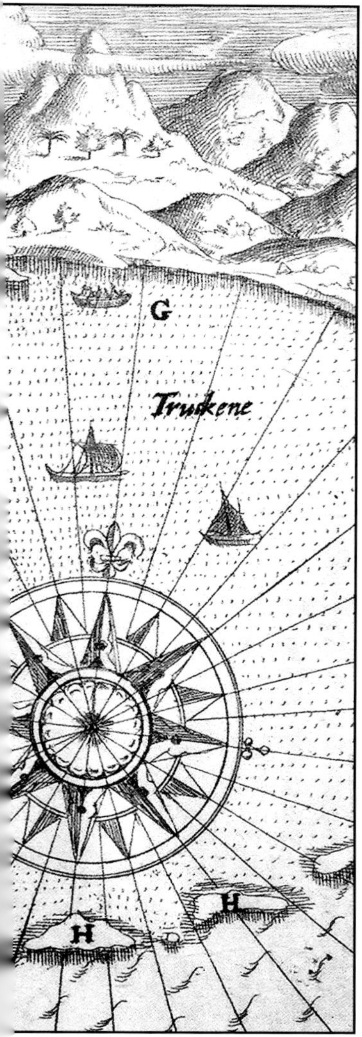

After the Portuguese, the Dutch, and then the English sailed the Indian Ocean. In 1600 the English established the East India Company and the Dutch followed suit.

The Dutch occupied the island twice, between 1638 and 1658 and then again from 1664 to 1710.

Cornelius Houtman commanded the first expedition that laid the foundation of the Dutch power in the region in 1595.

Admiral van Neck accompanied by Vice Admiral Wybrandt van Warwijck, landed on the Ilha do Cerne in 1598 and, 'after having ordered public thanks to be returned to God, for having conducted them to such a fair and secure harbour', the Admiral claimed the island for the Netherlands and named the island 'Mauritius' in honour of Maurice of Nassau, Prince of Orange (1567–1625), the Stadhouder of the seven Provinces of the Netherlands.

In the account of this voyage, the following description is given: 'On every side lofty mountains present themselves to the view, which are clothed with trees of the finest verdure, and whose summits are frequently enveloped with clouds, or dimly seen through floating mists. The soil is stony, but at the same time so entirely covered with wood, that it was impossible to force a passage through it. The wood is in general black, like the finest ebony, or of a very fine red, or a deep yellow, having the appearance of wax.'

The Moluccan Fleet led by Admiral Wolferst Harmensz and Vice Admiral Hans Hendricksz Bouwer, departed to the East Indies in 1601. It reached Mauritius in October and stayed there for three weeks to get water and provisions and to recover from scurvy. Many of the sailors that accompanied Harmensz had

The expedition of Wybrandt van Warwijck in Mauritius.

and that they saw there tortoises so
g, that four seamen sitting on the back
one of them, it went as well as if it
d had no burden at all. Where to they
ded, that they were so large, that ten
en might sit upon one shell.' *Travels*
o the Indies by J. A. Mandelslo, 1662.

le page of the book that contains the
yage of Jakob van Neck and Wybrandt
n Warwijck, 1598.

e of the Journal describing the
ounter with the French castaway.

already been on the island in 1598 under Wybrandt van Warwijck.

The short journal of Harmensz' trip includes a story of a marooned Frenchman, the only survivor of an unfortunate English expedition from 1596. This poor man had decided to stay in Mauritius until 'it should please Heaven to send relief'. He was 'left in solitude in this uninhabited spot' where he spent two years 'sustained with the fruit of the date tree and the flesh of turtles'.

The story of this sailor, included in John Albert de Mandelslo's book *Travels into the Indies* (1662) is said to have inspired Daniel Defoe's *Robinson Crusoe*.

'May the Almighty God give him back his health and may He protect us from such terrible misfortune, Amen', prayed the writer at the end of the report about this castaway.

After 1611, not only Dutch ships started calling at Mauritius, but French and English as well. It was easy to get supplies of fresh water and food there. Apart from that, the Dutch started felling ebony trees and gathering ambergris that they exported to Europe.

Ambergris is the substance found in the intestine of the sperm whale. In the East it was used as a spice, in the West to fix perfumes. It is often washed ashore or found floating free on the sea.

Willem Ysbrantsz Bontekoe, a Dutch seaman describes life on Mauritius: 'As the island is not inhabited, the sailors were free to wander over it, and so to amuse themselves with fishing, shooting or bird catching. They made wooden spits which served to roast the birds, and, by basting them with oil of turtles, they were rendered delicious food.'

In 1638 the Dutch East India Company sent an expedition to Mauritius in order to start a settlement in the south east corner of the island; its first governor was Cornelius Gooyer. The ruins of the Dutch fort can be seen at Vieux Grand Port (Frederik Hendrik Museum), near Mahébourg, where some of them have been excavated.

The south-eastern fort (H) and an English vessel (I), 1708.

The port on the west, proved to be the better one. Mandelslo describes it as follows: '...the Haven of it is very good, as well in regard, that at the entrance of it there is a hundred fathom water as that it is able to contain above fifty great Vessels, sheltered from all the winds. It hath some mountains which reaching up to clouds are seen at a great distance, and are extremely delightful to the eye, inasmuch as Nature maintains them in a constant verdure, though some Cocos–trees and Date trees only are expected, all the other trees are wild.'

Cornelius Gooyer was commissioned to make the necessary arrangements to meet all the demands of the vessels that called at Noord–Wester Haven.

After 1640 the first slaves started being introduced from Madagascar to help the settlers with the tobacco and sugar cane plantations and with the felling of ebony trees. Sugar cane had been introduced from Java together with deer and pigs.

In 1658, the Dutch evacuated the island and returned in 1664 to leave for good in 1710. The reason of their departure was that Mauritius did not have any commercial value for them, and ebony trees were no longer available.

From the two settlements, the Cape and Noord–Wester Haven, the Dutch preferred the Cape.

ast India Companies were British, utch and French commercial and olitical monopolistic organisations, at traded with the East Indies in tton, silk, indigo, saltpetre and spices.

1642, Abel Tasman (1603–1659) sailed om Mauritius to explore Tasmania, ji and New Zealand.

embers of the Warwijck expedition ding a giant tortoise.

Descriptive depiction of the first Dutch settlement.

The First Settlement

In 1601 Johann de Bry published a book containing accounts of travellers who visited the islands of the Indian Ocean. The print on the left, taken from that book is the first detailed record of a settlement in Mauritius.

Each number on the print has the original description that, although very naïve, is very close to the early, untouched island, that only the Dutch saw.

One has to bear in mind, that since the artist who created this picture was not part of the expedition, he had to base his engravings on the accounts of the travellers and not on his direct observation.

1. These are big tortoises, which just walk on the land because they can't swim. They eat crab, which they know how to catch and which are the size of a guinea pig. 2. This is a bird, which the Dutch call *walg* [*walg* means disgusting in Dutch]. It is the size of a swan and has a big head and a round body. Instead of wings it has only 3 or 4 little feathers. Instead of a tail it has only 3 or 4 crinkly feathers. They [the Dutch] cooked it but it was disgusting. 3. A palm tree which has big leaves. One leaf is enough to protect a man from rain. If a small hole is pierced in the tree, wine will flow out. It almost has the taste of Spanish wine. If it is kept for more than two days, it gets spoiled. They call it wine. 4. [This] Is a bird called *Rabos Forcados*. It has a tail that looks like the scissors of a tailor. They [the birds] are black, with a white breast and a long beak. They eat flying fish and when their offal was thrown into the sea, their companions ate it. 5. An Indian crow, twice the size of a parrot with two or three colours. 6. It is a wild tree, to which they [the Dutch] attached the coats of arms of Hollandt, Seelandt and Amsterdam as a symbol and as a reminder. 7. This is a *Palmites* tree. They cut the fruit marked with A which they ate against scurvy. The fruit tasted very good. 8. A bat that has the head the size of a macaque. Lots of them looking like the ones in the picture hung from the trees when they wanted to rest. 9. This is how the smith arranged his workshop. 10. Hut constructed by the Dutch with branches and leaves. They spent the nights there. 11. Spot where the sermon was given. Half of them in the morning and the other half listened to it in the afternoon. 12. With one cast they caught three half tons of fish.

The Pavillion, a giant tree described by Le Guat in 1691.

Rodrigues Island

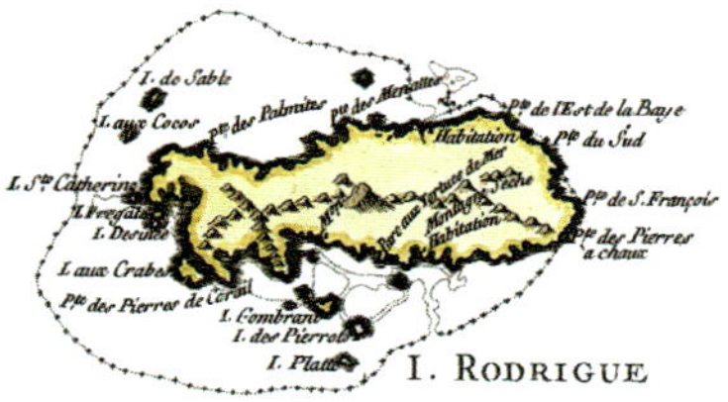

Nineteenth century map.

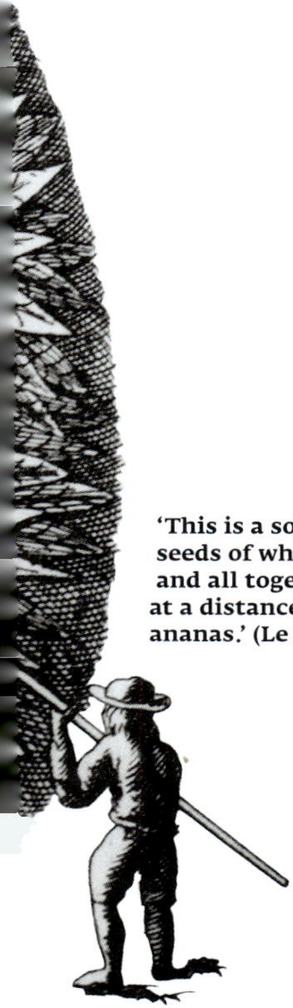

'This is a sort of grape, the seeds of which are close and all together. It looked at a distance like a fruit of ananas.' (Le Guat)

Rodrigues, originally called Diego Ruys Island, is the smallest of the Mascarene trio. It lies 560 km to the North of Mauritius, is of volcanic origin and is surrounded by a coral reef.

The Portuguese discovered Rodrigues in 1507 but they were not interested in occupying it. The Dutch settled it a century later, in 1601.

When the Dutch arrived, Rodrigues was covered by a thick forest, which has disappeared nowadays due to intensive grazing and cyclones. The Government of Mauritius is trying to nurse the endangered species to save them from extinction.

In 1691 a small advance party of a bigger expedition landed on this small island led by a man called François Le Guat who wrote a famous diary full of vivid descriptions of their sojourn.

'This little new world seemed to us a seat of delight; though we did not see so many birds as appeared on the shore of the Island Tristan, nor was the air so perfumed as when we passed the Isle of Bourbon, about a month before. But the aspect of this island was so delightful, that we could scarce satisfy ourselves with gazing at the little mountains of which it is composed, covered as they were with large and beautiful trees... The air of Rodrigues is very pure and wholesome; and as a proof of it, not one of us was sick during the two years we remained there, notwithstanding the great difference of climate and mode of nourishment'. (Le Guat)

Life on Rodrigues was like life in paradise but the party missed the company of women, so they decided to return to Mauritius, which was at that time, occupied by the Dutch.

As soon as they arrived at Mauritius, Le Guat and his companions were detained, accused of being

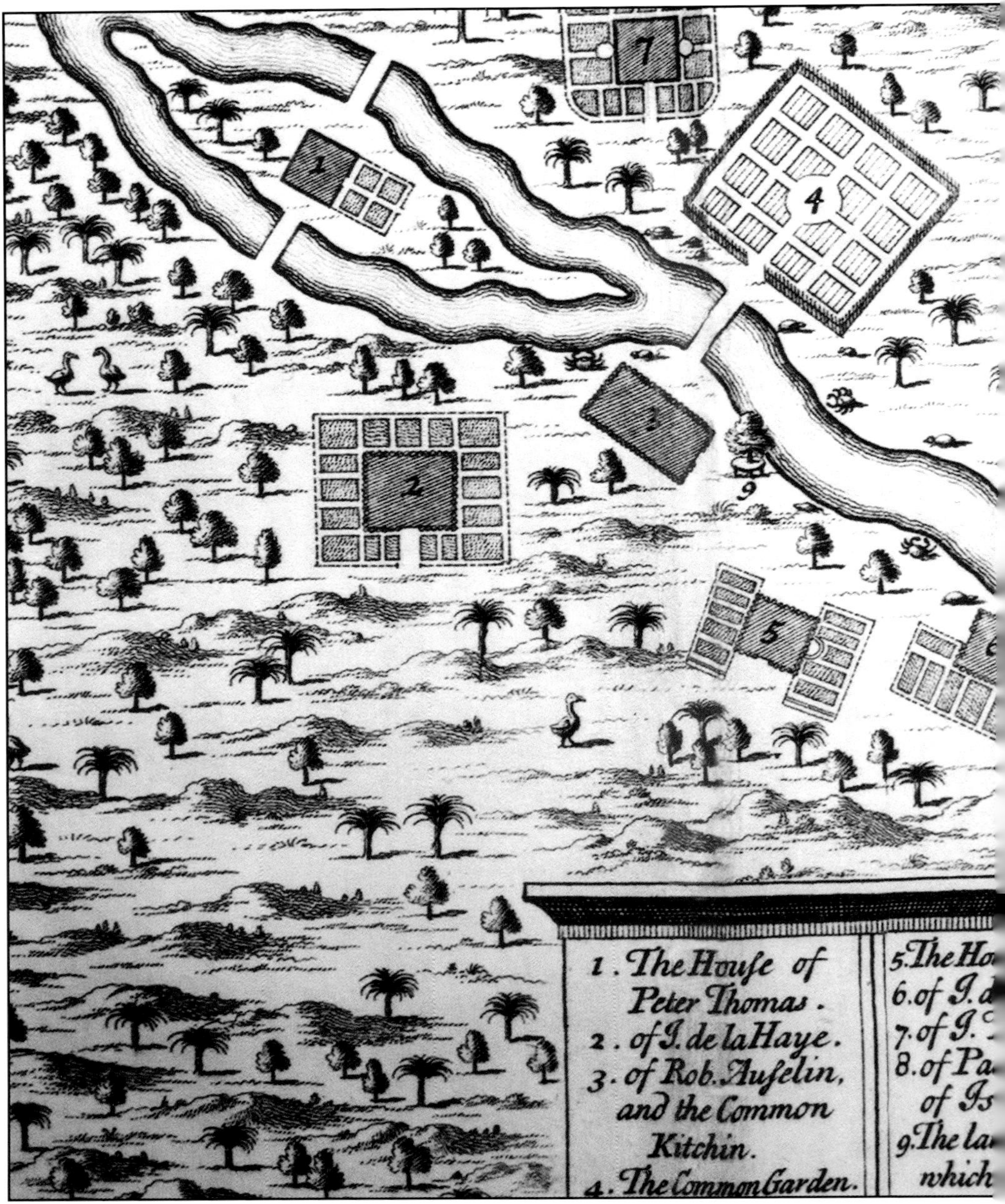

Plan of Le Guat's settlement.

8
MER
DES
INDES.

The Solitary.

spies. They were transferred to the small island of Batavia, where they spent almost three years. They only reached Holland in 1698.

The French, who were the next to arrive at Rodrigues, evacuated the island during the Napoleonic Wars. Since they devoted themselves to agriculture, they introduced slaves from Africa.

The British arrived in 1771 to stay for six months and returned in 1809 to assemble their troops to attack Mauritius, which was in French hands.

There are several small islands off the coast of Rodrigues: Île Cocos, the last refuge of the fody and the brush warbler; Île aux Sables, where noddies

and fairy terns are found; Île aux Chats, with a beautiful coral reef; Île aux Crabes and Île Hermitage, which according to tradition, has a buried treasure.

In the southwest corner of the island there is a rocky maze called Caverne Patate, a cavern with impressive stalagmite and stalactite formations.

Almost all inhabitants descend from the slaves who worked in the sugar cane plantations during the French colonisation. There are also Chinese and Indian immigrants. Most of the population are Roman Catholics. Their main occupations are fishing, agriculture, the production of handicrafts and tourism.

Rodrigues formerly a dependency of Mauritius became fully integrated as an electoral district in 1968. It sends members of parliament to the Mauritius Legislative Assembly. Today many Rodriguans migrate to Mauritius to work in the newly developed industries.

was sorry to leave Rodrigues; for from /hat I had seen of it, it seemed an nchanting and unspoiled island.' ;erald Durrell)

here is a wonderful fine tree in Rodrigo hose branches are so round and so hick, 'tis impossible for the sunbeams penetrate it. Some of these trees are big, that two or three hundred may tand under them and be shelter'd from he sun and the weather.' (Le Guat)

Guat's vessel in a storm off the shores Mauritius.

all the birds in the island, the most markable is that which goes by the me of Solitary, because he is very ldom seen in company, tho' there are undance of them.' (Le Guat)

The Dodo

The Dodo or Dronte, the big bird of Mauritius, (*Raphus cucullatus*, or *Didus ineptus*), makes up together with the *Raphus solitarius* of Réunion and the *Pezophaps solitaria* of Rodrigues, the family *Raphidae*.

This curious animal was discovered by the Portuguese in 1507 and was exterminated in the seventeenth century by the Dutch and the animals introduced by them: rats, monkeys and pigs. Today it is considered the world's most famous example of extinction.

Charles Grant in his *History of Mauritius* (1801) has a very detailed description of the Dodo:

'It commonly inhabits the island of Mauritius, so celebrated for the beautiful ebony wood which it produced. It is a very stupid animal: its size and figure is between that of the turkey and the ostrich; it is taller than a swan; its head is long, large, and shapeless; its feathers rise to a point on the forehead, and grow around the beak and on the face, in the form of a hood, from whence it has obtained the name of the hooded swan; its eyes are black and large; its beak which is strong, and of a considerable size and length, is both pointed and hooked, and of a pale blue colour; the neck is long, fat, and curved; the body is large and round, and covered with gray feathers, which are as soft as those of an ostrich; its wings are short; its legs are thick, long and of a yellow colour; it has four claws, three before and one behind; it does not fly and it is very slow in its progress when it walks: the flesh is covered with fat, and it is so nutritious, that three or four of these birds are sufficient to glut a hundred people.

'Stones are generally found in the stomach of this animal. Lightness and activity are attributes common to birds, but the Dodo has no claim to

Dodo sketched by a Dutch seaman in 160

For many years, the Dodo was thought to be a fantastic invention of sailors an travellers, but in 1865 the British scienti Charles Clark found a Dodo skeleton at Mare aux Songes. It was assembled in Edinburgh and a reconstruction of the Dodo can be seen in the Natural Histor Museum at Port Louis.

these characters; on the contrary, it appears to be expressly formed to give an idea of the heaviest of organized beings.

'Size, which in animals generally presupposes strength in this particular instance, produces nothing but weight. The ostrich, the tomjou, and the casoar are not more capable of flying than the Dodo; but they are very swift of foot; whereas, the Dodo appears to be borne down by its own weight, which it can scarce bear along.

'It may be said, indeed, to be composed of brute, inactive matter, in which the vivifying particles have been omitted: it has wings but they are too weak and too short, to lift it into the air; it has a tail but it is both disproportionate and out of its place.

ewis Carroll saw a model of the Dodo in xford and introduced the bird in Alice ı Wonderland. Illustration by Sir John enniel (1820–1914).

***e Dodo and Kindred Birds* by Roelandt ıvery, (1576–1639).**

It may be actually taken for a tortoise, covered with feathers and nature; by furnishing it with these useless ornaments, seems as if she wished to add the embarrassment to its natural weight, the awkwardness of its motions, to the inactivity of the mass, and render its lumpishness more disgusting, by forcing upon the observation that it is a bird.'

Cocotier by Édouard Pitot, 1865.

sle de France

ıe French who first established ıemselves there, were certain planters om the Isle of Bourbon, who brought ith them simplicity of manners, good ith, a hospitable disposition, and an difference for riches'. (Grant)

Captain Guillaume Dufresne d'Arsel (1688–1730) in an expedition in 1715 claimed the island of Mauritius for France and changed its name to 'Isle de France'. Noord–Wester Haven, the most important port on the island, also changed its name. From then on it was called Port Louis in honour of the French King Louis XV.

For a whole century the French used the Mascarene Islands as a base for ships on the Indian route, a place

with a safe port, where vessels could be repaired and where goods could be profitably traded because sugar cane, spices and coffee were successfully cultivated on the island. The arriving sailors were also fond of arak, a sort of rum prepared by the locals. In 1721, the first settlement was started by a party of colonists sent from the Isle of Bourbon (Réunion) and by a governor, soldiers and colonists who arrived from France. They also brought some slaves from Madagascar with them.

ıe East India Companies used agnificent ships called East Indiamen. ıey were highly gilded and decorated d were armed as warships for otection against pirates and warships other nations.

At the beginning the colony was administered from the Isle of Bourbon, but soon the seat of the government which was in the hands of the French East India Company, was transferred to the Isle of

t Louis is said to be 'the only point n the surface of the great Indian an […] upon which we would establish t to afford protection to our ımunications to India'. 'It is a safe and ımodious port accessible at all ıods of the year and to which ships run to avoid the terrible hurricanes ıis region.'

View of Port Louis, 1844.

Church in Pamplemousses, eighteenth century.

ahé de La Bourdonnais (1699–1753), rench School, eighteenth century.

France. The people in Bourbon usually complained that their position had been relegated to that of 'the granary of the Isle of France'.

After Governor Dufresne, de Nyon, de Brousse, Dumas and de Maupin followed. In 1735, the new Gouverneur–Général des Mascareignes, Bertrand François Mahé de La Bourdonnais arrived. He had been present in 1724 at the capture of the town of Mahé on the Malabar coast where he acted with such bravery that it is believed that it was named Mahé in his honour. His aspiration was to transform the island into a flourishing colony, and he certainly succeeded.

He was responsible for the harbour as a naval base, with new quays, forts for defence and warehouses, a new hospital, an aqueduct; he established a new road network, organised the first sugar cane factory at Rosalie and, above all, established internal order. To meet these necessities he not only recruited slaves in Mozambique, but brought qualified architects from Madras as well.

It was La Bourdonnais who chose Port Louis as the main port of the island. He knew that a port sheltered from the wind was easier to defend, because ships have to be towed into the port and they have a favourable wind to sail out.

La Bourdonnais is considered the best French governor the island ever had. His statue stands in the centre of Port Louis. Being an excellent naval commander, he was a good administrator. Monplaisir, the official Governor's residence in Pamplemousses, and a new Government House were built during his administration. In his garden at Pamplemousses, considered today one of the most beautiful botanical gardens in the world, he experimented on vegetables which were to be grown on the Isle of France in order to spread the cultivation of food crops. He even introduced manioc from South America: food shortage had always been one of the threats of the island.

'M. de La Bourdonnais, that great man, whom history already mentions with eulogiums which he so well deserves, that great general, mariner,

View of Port Louis.

administrator, merchant, and agriculturist, entertained very different opinions; his knowledge of it was the result of several years passed in the government of it, and to him it is indebted for the sources of its prosperity: he considered the Isle of France as the key of the Indian commerce of his nation, as the bulwark of its settlements in Asia, and as the means of future conquests.' (de Cossigny)

.mplemousses by J. G. Milbert, 1812.

La Bourdonnais was succeeded by Martin, David and then by de Lozier–Bouvet who was responsible for the law concerning a closer supervision of slaves, who were accused of 'devoting all their efforts to escaping'. In 1764, after the governors Magon and Desforges–Boucher, the administration of the island passed from the hands of the French East India Company into those of the French King. This was the time of the famous French pirates and corsairs who ravaged the Indian Ocean until 1810. Some of the most famous corsairs were Carosin, Drieu, Dutertre, Garneray, Le Même, Perroud and Robert Surcouf. Port Louis became haven for them and the booty of Portuguese and British ships sold there attracted many merchants from all over the world.

1744, during the administration of La urdonnais, one of the best-known storic events of Mauritius occurred: e *Saint-Géran* tragedy, which inspired rnardin de Saint Pierre to write his nous novel, *Paul et Virginie*.

Paul & Virginie

Jacques Henri Bernardin de Saint Pierre's first work was *Voyage à l'Isle de France*, a collection of vivid letters where his descriptive talent is already announced.

He is without doubt an early forerunner of the Romantic Movement. As Rousseau's most important follower in his back–to–nature philosophy, this French writer is famous for his novel *Paul et Virginie*, set in an idyllic and unspoiled scenery in what was called, at that time, Isle of France.

Paul et Virginie is the story of two children who live together since early childhood. They love each other and after a separation, want to meet again and marry. A catastrophe, which is presented as an interference of civilisation, destroys their happiness.

This novel is an illustration of de Saint Pierre's utopian dream. He presents the relationship of 'natural beauty in the tropics and the moral beauty of a small community'. His writing evokes the magnificent scenery of the island of Mauritius, where these two children naturally ignore evil.

'...the rock was left as it had been decorated by nature. On its brown and moist sides broad plants of maiden–hair glistened with their green and dark stars; and tufts of wave–leaved hart's tongue, suspended like long ribbons of purpled green, floated on the wind. Near this grew a chain of the Madagascar periwinkle, the flowers of which resemble the red gilliflower; and peppers, the seed–vessels of which are of the colour of blood, and more resplendent than coral. Near them, the herb balm, with its heart–shaped leaves, and the sweet basil, which has the odour of the clove, exhaled the most delicious perfumes. From the precipitous side of the mountain hung the graceful lianas, like floating draperies, forming magnificent canopies of verdure

Portraits of Paul and Virginie.

on the face of the rocks. The seabirds, allured by the stillness of these retreats, resorted here to pass the night. At the hour of sunset we could perceive the curlew and the stint skimming along the seashore; the frigate bird poised high in air; and the white bird of the tropic, which abandons, with the star of day, the solitudes of the Indian Ocean.'

Their happiness 'consisted in living according to nature and according to virtue', but civilisation will disrupt their happiness.

Paul et Virginie is based on a real tragedy: a ship called *Saint-Géran* shipwrecked off the Île d'Ambre in 1744 and two women were drowned because they refused to take off their clothes and were not able to swim with the weight of them.

In the Blue Penny Museum in Port Louis, a sculpture by Prosper d'Epinay (1836–1914) represents the ill-fated lovers.

ernardin de Saint Pierre (1737–1814).

fter a trip to different parts of the orld, Bernardin de Saint Pierre spent vo years on the Isle of France. In 1773 e published *Voyage à l'Isle de France* a ostalgic account of a lost paradise. In 84 he wrote *Études de la nature*, to which e added in 1788 the love story of *Paul et rginie*.

ost of these trees shed aromatic odours powerful, that the garments of a aveller, who has passed through the rest, often retain for hours the most licious fragrance.' *Paul et Virginie*.

Corsairs and Pirates

Corsairs were mercenary marines with an official permission and paid by a country to plunder the ships of enemy nations. Pirates had no license whatsoever; they just attacked any ship of any nation.

Robert Surcouf, the 'King of Corsairs' was born in St Malo, France. He was one of the most famous privateer captains of the Indian Ocean. He started his career when he was 13 and became an officer when he was 17. Surcouf made slaving voyages to Mozambique and operated in the Bay of Bengal, making many captures of British ships. In 1807, he built in St Malo the famous large three-masted *Revenant* and started a new campaign in the Indian Ocean.

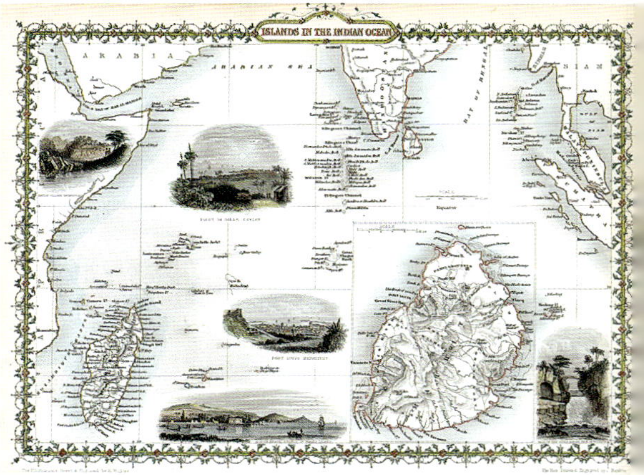

Islands in the Indian Ocean by Winkles and Rapkin (1850).

Destruction of the frigate *La Preneuse* at the Baie du Tombeau, Mauritius, 11 December 1799

Royal Rule

Pierre Poivre (1719–1786).

Between 1764 and 1790 the Isle of France was under the rule of an intendant, who represented the King with powers in justice and finance, and a governor with military and naval authority. It was a time of prosperity and growth. Port Louis was called 'Paris of the Indian Ocean'.

The first and probably best intendant sent by the crown, was Pierre Poivre, who tried and partly succeeded in organising a better life on the island. He insisted on growing spice plants: pepper, cinnamon, cloves and nutmeg.

People were also encouraged to grow coffee, sugar cane, cotton, indigo and tea. Sugar cane was going to be the most important good exported from the Isle of France.

The name Moka, a town in the centre of the island, 'was originally given to it from the excellence of the coffee grown there, as resembling that sold in England from Mocha.'

The governors sent to the island after Poivre were Dumas, Steinauer, des Roches, Ternay, la Brillane, de Souillac, Narbonne, d'Entrecasteaux and Cossigny.

During the wars of 1778 and 1783 and as a consequence of the prosperity of the island, many ships visited Port Louis. The cultivation of sugar cane had spread, indigo was grown, spirits were manufactured, and French corsairs, who kept raiding British ships in the Indian Ocean, brought the goods to the Isle of France.

Pepper, coffee & sugar cane.

Sugar cane fields.

The west of Port Louis from the harbour, 1813.

rench Revolution

When the news of the French Revolution reached the remote Isle of France, the inhabitants were confused and could not understand what was happening in France. Each ship brought varied details about the ideas behind the revolution and the news were always several months late. Eventually, a general assembly, later called Colonial Assembly, and several district and municipal councils were set up. A National Guard was created. The restrictions of the Code Noir, were temporarily lifted and the name of the Isle of Bourbon was changed into that of Réunion. There was only one victim of the French Revolution on the island: a royalist naval officer called Mac Namara, who was killed by a mob in Port Louis.

The revolutionary authorities in France appointed General Anne Joseph Hippolyte de Malartic (1730–1800) as the new governor. He was commissioned to ensure that the ideas of the revolution were carried out on the island. He cooperated with the planters and tried to spare the island from disorder.

When in 1796 a naval force under the command of de Sercey arrived to enforce the law that abolished slavery (which had been passed in Paris, in 1794), the inhabitants of the Isle of France rebelled. On this topic, they all were of the same opinion: if 88% of the inhabitants of the island were slaves, then it would be 'very dangerous' to set them all free and at the same time. The islanders defied the law, and during almost four years, until Charles Mathieu Isidore Decaen was appointed as the highest authority in 1803, the Isle of France was an independent territory protected only by corsairs who found a suitable base at Port Louis.

The political scene changed altogether with the ascent of Napoleon. Decaen allowed slavery to

Badamier (*Terminalia badamia*) by Édouard Pitot, 1865.

athew Flinders (1774–1814) had been
mmissioned to explore and chart the
ıstralian coast. On his voyage back to
ıgland, the bad condition of his ship
ade him put in at Port Louis in 1803.
e was interned by the French as a
isoner of war and had to remain in
auritius until 1810.

continue, abolished the Colonial Assembly and the councils, replaced the National Guard by a legion, renamed Port Louis, Port Napoleon (Réunion was renamed Bonaparte Island) and the Napoleonic Codes started being used on the island.

Commerce flourished on the Isle of France during Decaen's government.

British ships continued to be captured by French corsairs in the Indian Ocean. The British, tired of these attacks, blockaded the Isle of France. It was then that the British explorer and naturalist Mathew Flinders was imprisoned.

In 1809 a British fleet was sent from Bombay and the Cape and occupied the island of Rodrigues. In 1810 the fleet took the island of Réunion. It was from Réunion that General Abercrombie set off to capture the Isle of France.

ı–Palm or Tallipot by Édouard Pitot,
5.

p of the Isle of France, 1836.

Combat du Grand Port by Mayer.

Battle of Grand Port

A few ships of the French Navy defended the Isle of France during the Napoleonic Wars. In August 1810, a British squadron attacked the French Fleet at the entrance to Vieux Grand Port and suffered a defeat after a three day battle. This is the only French naval victory inscribed on the Triumphal Arch in Paris. Both commanders, Captain Victor Guy Duperré and Captain Willoughby, were wounded during the battle and were treated side by side in the chateau Robillard in Mahébourg.

In November, the British landed with 70 ships and 10 000 troops at Cap Malheureux, on the northern coast of the Isle of France.

On 3 December, Governor Charles Decaen, surrendered to the British and negotiated a very honourable capitulation. The long struggle for the supremacy in the Indian Ocean had come to an end.

The engraving on the left shows the battle of Grand Port on 25 August 1810. The frigates *Bellone*, *Minerve*, *Ceylon* and *Victor* combat and destroy an English division of four vessels.

***Combat du Grand Port*, 24 August 1810.**

***British Army Landing (29 November 1810)* by Temple, 1813.**

British Arrival

The Treaty of Paris in 1814 gave the Isle of France, together with Rodrigues and the Seychelles to the British and returned the island of Réunion to the French.

British occupation made only little difference to the lifestyle led by the people on the island. They could retain their language, their religion, their Napoleonic Code and their customs and no new colonists were introduced.

The British made two changes: they changed the name of the island back to 'Mauritius' and they established their own government. The British had taken the islands only for strategic reasons: they wanted to put an end to the activities of the corsairs who used to take refuge in Port Louis. Lord Chatham (William Pitt) had once said: 'As long as the French hold the Isle of France, the British will never be masters of India'.

But soon the first difficulty arose. The British Parliament had passed the 'Act for the Abolition of the Slave Trade' in 1807, the question of slave abolition was an important topic in Britain and Mauritius was part of the Empire.

The first British Governor of Mauritius, Robert Farquhar, faced a dilemma under the terms of the 1810 capitulation. The British Government had guaranteed that French customs and lifestyle were to be kept on the island yet slavery had been forbidden throughout the British Empire.

Mauritius was at that time expanding its sugar cane plantations and it needed extra labour to clean the fields from lava boulders and to plant and harvest the cane.

Apart from that, planters regarded slaves as their property and they considered it their inalienable right, to own slaves. If slavery was to be abolished, then a compensation had to be paid.

The Franco–Mauritians organised a political committee in 1827, the Comité Colonial. Its members were delegates from the various districts of the island representing the planters, and the lawyer Adrien Antoine d'Épinay (1794–1839), became its leader and spokesman.

The Comité sent him to London, to fight for the rights of the planters and to force the British to pay compensation if slavery had to be abolished. He also intended to give the Franco–Mauritians a place in the Council of Government which had been set up in 1825 under Governor Cole.

This Council was made up of the Chief of Justice, the Chief Secretary, the Commanding Officer of the

After signing the treaty with the British, Louis XVIII said: 'You keep the port and leave us the volcano'.

***Vue de la Citadelle du Port Louis* by Bouquet, 1838.**

Garrison and the Controller of Customs. The Council was thus made up of members who were elected only because of the office or position they held.

In 1832, the British government sent John Jeremie to Mauritius to take up a legal post. Since the planters knew that he was a well known abolitionist, a general strike was organised in Port Louis. The Governor, anxious to keep order, asked Jeremie to leave. The planters had succeeded once again.

British Governors did not lead an easy life in Mauritius, for it was difficult to resist the planters. If they did, their life on the island became unpleasant and complicated, and sometimes, they were even forced to resign.

Soon after and as an answer to this insurrection, the British built a citadel, called Fort Adelaide, which overlooks the capital, in order to be able to control possible revolts among its inhabitants.

When the second constitution was introduced under Governor Charles Colville, some changes were made in the composition of the council. It was going to be made up of 15 members: the governor, who was its president, seven colonial officials and seven members appointed by the governor and chosen from the influential chief land owners and

he One Penny Red and Two Pence Blue, re among the most expensive stamps in ne world due to an alleged error ('Post ffice' instead of 'Post Paid'), both can e seen in the Blue Penny Museum in ort Louis.

Port Louis, about one mile distant from the shore, 1813.

he shrine of Père Jacques Désiré Laval
the 'Lourdes of the Indian Ocean'. He
as beatified by Pope John Paul II in 1979.

arieties of mangoes from Mauritius,
atercolours, 1845.

merchants of the colony. Adrien Antoine d'Épinay formed part of this council.

In 1833, £ 2 million were paid to the slave owners as compensation and slavery was abolished in February 1835.

The emancipated slaves were forced by law to go on working as paid labourers on the plantations of their former owners, for four years. Finally, in 1839, all slaves left the plantations. Most of them started working as fishermen or became smallholders and started new settlements.

Ex–slaves did not get much help from their former owners once they had been set free. Only two priests, Father Jean Lebrun (1789–1865) and Father Jacques Désiré Laval (1803–1864) helped them find a new position in society.

Since sugar industry was expanding and slavery had been abolished, the planters started looking for new labourers from other colonies.

The solution was promptly determined by the British government: they allowed the planters to bring workers from India, China, Mozambique and Madagascar under the indentured system.

This indentured system tied the labourer to fixed wage contracts; if the labourer refused to work, then he could be imprisoned. The treatment the labourers received resembled that of the slaves. When the Commissions of Enquiry were sent from Britain to investigate on labour conditions, their reports were usually disapproving.

In the following seventy years a massive immigration was going to change the island's population radically.

Immigrants

Mauritian society is nowadays composed of a majority of people of Indian origin (Hindus in a bigger proportion than Muslims), about 30% are of mixed Creole origin, a 3% is of Chinese origin and a small part (1.3%) is of French origin.

Until the seventeenth century, Mauritius was an uninhabited island and its society has been shaped exclusively by immigration. Only under such different administrations (Dutch, French and English) and because of the island's location, it is possible to understand the development of such a colourful society.

Indian labour has an extensive history in Mauritius. It started with the early settlements of the Dutch. There are records that indicate that already in 1638 South Asians were introduced as slaves to work on the island.

When the French took over, more Indians were introduced, principally from Pondicherry and other French colonies. At that time, the first free immigrants arrived. They were skilled South Indian artisans.

Towards 1750, society in the Isle of France was composed of Guineés, Malays, Tamils, Bengalis and French settlers.

Mozambican and Malagasy slaves were introduced with the first organised slave-trading voyages and very quickly outnumbered all other groups. To regulate the introduction of slaves, legislation had to be passed. The compilation of laws regarding slave's work on the island was the so-called Code Noir. Society was legally split into whites, free blacks and slaves, and although relationships that crossed these divisions became illegal, informal unions were widespread.

'I have seen, every day, men and women being whipped because they had broken some pottery, forgotten to close a door. I have seen them bleeding and being rubbed with vinegar and salt to heal their wounds.

I have seen them at the port, in the excess of their pain, without being able to cry, bite the canon to which they had been tied to.

My feather is tired of writing these horrors, my eyes are weary of seeing and my ear of hearing them.' Bernardin de Saint Pierre, 1773.

Slaves on the Isle of France, J. M. Moreau, 1772.

'I am a man and nothing that belongs to mankind is alien to me', B. de Saint Pierre.

After the French Revolution, slave emancipation movements grew stronger. In 1835, with the abolition of slavery and under British rule, a system of indentured labour was introduced. The freed Creole population moved to coastal areas while new Indian immigrants formed busy villages around the plantations. The geographical movements of these groups were followed by traders and artisans who opened shops in the new settlements.

Wedgwood cameo used as anti-slavery propaganda.

Freed slaves from Mozambique, 1864.

In the following years the abuses with Indian indentured labour were criticised and denounced in the British Parliament and press, and the introduction of Indian labour had to be stopped between 1839 and 1842. During this period, sugar exports fell dramatically and a new indentured labour system was introduced in 1843. Under this system, which lasted until 1910, around half a million Indians arrived at the Mauritian shores. Vessels crowded with Indian labourers and families departed mainly from Calcutta, Madras and Bombay to establish themselves in the colony.

'Before seeing these people I had no ide that the inhabitants of India were suc noble looking men; their skin is extremely dark, and many of the older men had large moustachios and beard of a snow white colour; this, together with the fire of their expressions, gave to them an aspect quite imposing.'
Charles Darwin (Mauritius, 1836)

By the end of the nineteenth century, the low price of sugar and a series of natural catastrophes that affected the sugar cane production, made the whites abandon its cultivation. In the 1880s, the big

dian immigrant as recorded in the gistry for labourers.

migrants from India identified emselves as Christian, Hindu and ıslim. Within the Hindu community, ınicity and caste created further ɒgroups.

plantations were sold off to Indian smallholders. This was called the *grand morcellement* (literally: great partition) and marked a crucial step in the rise of Indian leadership in Mauritius.

The history of Chinese immigration to Mauritius follows a different track. Governor Farquhar introduced the first free Chinese immigrants under British rule. Chinese traders, particularly Fukienese and Cantonese established their shops in the bigger towns, especially in Port Louis. In the 1850s, after the Taiping revolution, the Hakkas were forced to leave China and some arrived in Mauritius. They quickly outnumbered all other Chinese people. The Chinese, who mixed with the local population, form the sino-mauritian group.

Indian immigrants in the village of Antoinette, 1862.

Creole

Creole is the name given to any language that has evolved from the fusion of languages spoken in Africa and languages spoken by other ethnic groups during colonisation. All countries, in which Creole is spoken, had plantations and a multicultural society.

In Mauritius, Creole, also spelled *Kreol*, is an adaptation and simplification of French enriched with words and speech patterns from the languages spoken by the different communities that speak it. This fascinating and colourful language, that has become the lingua franca of the island, is spoken by almost everyone. Although it is not taught at school, (it has no official written form), Creole is not considered the language of the uneducated and is spoken at all levels and situations.

Government forms, road signs, tourism, commerce and business are carried out in English (the country's official language); newspapers, magazines, radio, TV programmes, shop signs and street names, are in French. Creole, which started not later than 1770, is the means of oral communication.

It is a simple, flexible language: verbs are not conjugated, nouns have no plurals and it has a very simple syntax.

Most of the French words have been shortened and articles and adjectives have been merged to nouns so that the words are not easily recognisable, not even to French speakers. This merging of words has resulted in making Creole sound 'faster' than French.

Seventy five percent of the words are of French origin and some have even retained the meaning they had in the eighteenth century, when the French settled Mauritius. Creole is a living language, ready to adopt words whenever they are needed.

MUSIQUE
MUSIK
MISIK

Kreol doesn't have any grammar and words can be spelled in different ways.

There are hardly any words from Dutc in Kreol (the Mauritian French Creole) but there are words from Bantu (a larg group of languages spoken by the peoples of South and Central Africa), Hindi, Tamil, Bhojpuri, Swahili, Malagasy, Chinese and English.

Pidgin is not the native language of ar of its speakers, it is just a language us in order to communicate in work oriented situations. The word pidgin i the corruption of the word business. Creole is the native language of its speakers and has a more elaborate grammatical system than pidgin.

ng with Kreol, ethnic groups still learn their ancestral languages.

;ega

ıe most famous *ségatiers* are, among hers Ti Frère, Serge Lebrasse, Claudio, ɔger Clency and his wife Marie–Josée ıd Babalé.

ːga Typique', traditional or classical ːga has almost disappeared nowadays. ːga Salon' is danced in the houses. ːga Hotel' is the colourful, choreo- aphed, rehearsed and thus less sensual ıow that tourists enjoy in hotels.

Sega has its origin in the fertility rites brought from Africa by the slaves as early as the eighteenth century. It is usually associated with the Rivière Noire (Black River), a district on the western coast of Mauritius where the runaway slaves (*esclaves marrons*) used to hide.

Tired of their day's labour, the slaves met around a fire on the beach. There they drank their make shift rum, sang their sorrows and danced to the beats of their tambours.

These meetings on the beach were called *tchéga*, a Bantu word meaning play or dance. The word sega probably derives from *tchéga*.

Sega is a courtship dance accompanied by texts in Kreol, which usually have sexually undertoned puns. It is never obscene, the partners never even touch each other. They just swing and rock to the powerful beat of the drum and since it was danced on the beach, the feet never leave the ground. The drumbeats start slowly and then, little by little they build up to a crescendo, ending in a frenzied climax.

Three simple musical instruments accompany the Sega. The ravanne is a simple goatskin drum. The maravanne is a wooden box filled with dried seeds, which is shaken to get a scratchy sound. The triang is an iron triangle, which is beaten with a piece of metal. Cooking pots, pans, spoons and seedpods used as rattles and empty bottles are sometimes used for want of better instruments. Today, modern *ségatiers* also use guitars and keyboards.

Sega has achieved a widespread popularity nowadays and its success arises from its strong rhythm, its catchy tunes and its expression of happiness. It is difficult to resist the excitement of its rhythm.

The Caudan Waterfront, Port Louis.

Towards a New Political Order

In 1853 a new powerful and effective pressure group, the Chamber of Agriculture, was established. It was controlled by planters who still exercised great influence on the island.

Mauritius did not have an elected legislative council until 1885 when a new Constitution was introduced.

During the Governorship of Sir John Pope Hennessy (1883–1889), two lawyers became the leaders of the Reform Movement: William Newton and Virgile Naz. They both were plantation owners and wanted more power in government through a more direct share in the election of the unofficial members of the Council of Government.

The number of the members of the council was eventually increased from 14 to 27, eight official members, nine nominated members and ten elected unofficial members (one from each rural district and two from Port Louis). But the Indians still did not have their representatives. Mahatma Gandhi visited Mauritius in 1901 to help push for their civil rights.

In 1905 two political parties were organised, the Action Libérale and the Parti de l'Ordre. The Indian barrister Manilal Doctor, member of the Action Libérale party, tried to move the Indian community out of its apathy.

Several ideas about the future of Mauritius were put forward at that time: some thought that the island could be linked politically with India, others started a campaign to restore Mauritius to France again. The latter was called the 'Retrocession Movement'.

Dr Maurice Curé started a campaign and in 1936 launched the Labour Party to fight for the rights of the labourers and it grew in strength during the

1950s under the leadership of Dr Seewoosagur Ramgoolam, who became the official spokesman of the Indians.

Dr Seewoosagur Ramgoolam studied in Britain and returned to Mauritius in 1935. He was then elected member of the Port Louis Municipal Council and in 1940 was nominated by the governor, Sir Bede Clifford, to replace one of the two Indians on the Council of Government where he advocated for universal suffrage. He would be the leading person in the fight for Independence.

Moderate and tolerant, he was committed to encourage national unity and the creation of a welfare state. He died in 1985 at the age of 85.

The economic, administrative and political reforms which were introduced at that time and several external events helped the people in Mauritius attain self government. In 1968, Mauritius finally gained its Independence.

The brothers Basdeo and Sookdeo Bissoondoyal played a prominent role in the cultural, religious and political emancipation of the Hindus. Basdeo Bissoondoyal, who had studied in India, returned to Mauritius in 1939 and founded the Jan Andolan movement. His objectives were to make Hindus of diverse backgrounds aware and proud of their common cultural heritage. In 1943 a huge crowd celebrated the Maha Jag in Port Louis in perfect order.

After the Labour Party had won elections in Britain and India had been granted her independence in 1947, Britain started a different policy with her colonies. It had become very difficult for her to stop the nationalistic movements in all her colonies after the Second World War.

In 1947 a British commission proposed that the vote in Mauritius should be extended to all those who were able to read and write simple sentences in any of the languages used on the island. Nearly two thirds of the population of Mauritius could then vote and the elections of 1948 marked a point of inflection in the constitutional history of the island. For the

Mahatma Gandhi (1864–1948).

first time the nominated and official members in the Council were outnumbered by elected members.

The following elections of 1953 and 1959 carried democracy a step further.

New political parties were created, older ones changed their names, some of them formed coalitions, most of them pursued the same aim: the Independence of Mauritius.

The Parti Mauricien Social Démocrate (PMSD) with Gaetan Duval who was going to be a leading personality in this party, the Comité d'Action Musulmane (CAM), the Independent Forward Block (IFB) led by Sookdeo Bissoondoyal, were the parties that entered elections in 1959.

Two Constitutional Conferences took place in London, in 1961 and in 1965. In 1962 Ramgoolam was appointed Chief Minister and in 1967, Mauritius became self-governing.

'he types of Mauritius: Chinese rader, Muslim priest, Malagassy rover, Indian labourer.

Colonial house in 1860.

Architecture

'offee on the verandah, a deliciously
resh air and bright moonlight; there
re moments that repay one for a
ropical midday; the evening and the
arly morning are divine and to see the
eople sitting listlessly in their deep
hairs giving themselves up entirely to
he soft languor that then creeps over
ne, you would think them the most
areless beings on earth, as in one
ense, perhaps they are...'
engal civilian, 1838.

Mauritian houses immediately seduce the visitors because they epitomize what the traveller imagines, was the lifestyle of the Europeans in the tropics.

They were conceived with certain distinctive features to solve the problems presented by the wet, hot and ever–changing climate of the island.

The sloping roofs designed to cope with heavy rains, are covered by shingles or, as a precaution against fire hazards, corrugated iron. These tall roofs create a space of cool air, which protects the living area from the heat; the windows in the roof provide ventilation to dry the dampness that condensates in the attic.

Shingles made of resilient wood of the tamarind are painted with a mixture of bitumen, ash from madrepore and permanganate that renders them waterproof and keeps away hungry termites.

During the French settlement, the roofs made by naval carpenters, resembled hulls turned upside down. British influence replaced these long roofs by a row of attic windows, and two turrets were symmetrically added at both ends.

Windows and doors are placed in such a way that the breeze can circulate through the house and provide refreshing ventilation. All rooms are thus intercommunicated. Usually, several doors open to the veranda, to give the dwellers direct access to the rooms of the house.

The elevated veranda, called *varangue* by the Mauritians, runs on one or more sides of the house, and more often than not, it surrounds the house completely. Here, in the best lit place of the house, the heat is bearable. In order to protect the living quarters from the sun, raffia blinds are lowered to filter the light. Comfortable chairs and a profusion

Temple in Port Louis.

The lace-like trimmings that line roofs, windows and the canopies above the doors (called *auvents*) are carved wooden borders usually painted in white, which show the craftsmanship and imagination of local carpenters.

of plants help make the veranda the favourite place of the house; here visitors are received.

At the beginning, the French settlers built the walls of wood planks or used layers of leaves of

House at Moka Hill, by J. G. Milbert, 1812.

ravenala tree. The British prepared a stone foundation into which they placed the wooden construction. Since these planks could be dismantled, many houses in Mauritius were moved and rebuilt somewhere else.

These houses are unlike any other in the world and it is hoped that they will be preserved as a unique heritage.

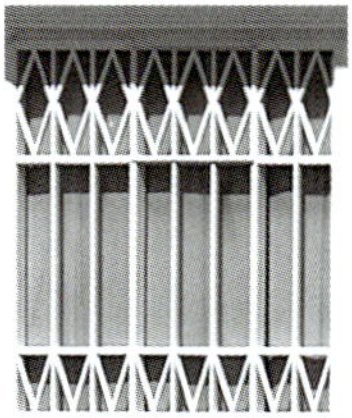

A large glass window cannot resist the force of a cyclone so small paned doors and windows are used instead.

Colonial house in Forest Side, Curepipe.

Independence & Republic

On 22 August 1967, Sir Seewoosagur Ramgoolam presented the following resolution to be forwarded by the Assembly:

'This Assembly requests Her Majesty's Government in the United Kingdom to take the necessary steps to give effect, as soon as practicable this year, to the desire of the people of Mauritius to accede to Independence within the Commonwealth of Nations and that Mauritius be admitted to Membership of the Commonwealth on the attainment of Independence.'

Sir Seewoosagur Ramgoolam's words during the debate were: 'We are meeting today on a historic and solemn occasion. By our decision today we shall put Mauritius on the path of her destiny. It is a day of joy for all patriotic men and women, for on this day we are taking the formal step which will confer on our people and bring them into their heritage... We have striven for many years now to create a new sense of unity out of our rich diversity and in the words of the poet let it be said for the glory of those who are fortunate to live at this hour: "Bliss was it in that dawn to be alive".'

Mauritius was finally granted independence from Britain on 12 March 1968. Sir Seewoosagur Ramgoolam was elected prime minister and he remained in office for the next 13 years.

Political life in Mauritius after independence was marked by a series of coalitions of the four principal political parties. These coalitions sometimes broke

The Coat of Arms of Mauritius. The motto reads 'Star and key of the Indian Ocean'.

Sir Seewoosagur Ramgoolam (1900–1985).

The four principal parties are the Labour Party, the Mouvement Militant Mauricien (MMM), the Mouvement Socialiste Mauricien (MSM) and the Parti Mauricien Social Démocrate (PMSD).

up, were changed and some survived.

The country was still economically on shaky grounds in the wake of independence and a turning point in the fortune started in 1982 when Sir Anerood Jugnauth took office for the first time. He was prime minister (1982–1995, 2000–2003) and president (2003) of Mauritius.

'rime Ministers since independence:
968–1982 Sir Seewoosagur Ramgoolam
982–1995 Sir Anerood Jugnauth
995–2000 Navin Ramgoolam
000–2003 Sir Anerood Jugnauth
003– 2005 Paul Bérenger
005 Navin Ramgoolam

After qualifying as a barrister in London, he returned to Mauritius and in 1963 was elected to the Legislative Council in the period before independence. In 1982 he became prime minister at the head of an alliance between the PSM (Mauritian Socialist Party) and the MMM from which he later broke away to form his own party.

In 1983 he created the MSM (Mauritian Socialist Movement), with a pledge to make the country a republic within the Commonwealth. The 1991 election gave his ruling coalition sufficient majority to pass the bill to sever ties with the British monarchy. In 1992, prime minister Jugnauth was the driving force behind Mauritius becoming a republic, while remaining a member of the Commonwealth and the Queen was replaced as head of state by a locally nominated president. He is the author of the economic miracle of Mauritius, which nowadays is one of Africa's most successful democracies and has enjoyed years of constitutional order.

Nowadays, Mauritius shares a special relationship with many eastern and western countries and in addition to its sugar mono-crop economy, has been able to diversify in a variety of sectors such as textiles, port services, IT and up-market tourism. Always looking for new challenges, Mauritius is now building hi–tech facilities for companies and aims to become a Cyber-island, making sure that it always remains, the key and star of the Indian Ocean.

Chronology

Before the fifteenth century Arab traders sighted Mauritius, called it Dina Mozare but did not settle it.

1638 The island was used as a supply base for Java. The ruins of this settlement can be visited near Mahébourg at the northern end of Vieux Grand Port.

1691 The expedition led by François Leguat arrived at Rodrigues.

1715 Captain Guillaume Dufresne d'Arsel annexed Mauritius to France and renamed the island Isle de France. It was given to the French East India Company as a trading base.

1721 The French occupatio began. Slaves were brought from Madagasca Mozambique and Asia to work in the sugar plantations.

1500

1650

1492 The Portuguese discovered the island in the wake of Vasco da Gama's trip around the Cape of Good Hope.

1507 Domingo Fernández Pereira dropped anchor at Mauritius and named the island Ilha do Cerne.

1528 The Portuguese Diego Rodríguez discovered an island to the east of Mauritius and gave the island his name.

1598 Vice Admiral Wybrandt van Warwyck landed on the south east coast of Mauritius and claimed the island for the Netherlands. He named it Mauritius after the Dutch Governor Maurice of Nassau, Prince of Orange.

1639 The Dutch introduced sugar cane and deer imported from Indonesia into the island.

1710 The Dutch abandoned Mauritius.

1735 to 1747 Mahé de La Bourdonais was appointe Governor of the Mascaren Islands.

1744 The *Saint-Géran* trage took place off the île d'Ambre.

764 The French East India :ompany handed over the sland to the French King.

303 General Decaen, the ıst French governor of the ;land, was designated.

;10 Battle of Vieux Grand ɔrt. The British took over ıe island.

1843 Indentured labour from India was introduced.

1901 Mahatma Gandhi visited Mauritius.

1936 The Labour Party was founded.

1968 Independence. Sir Seewoosagur Ramgoolam became Prime Minister.

1992 The Republic was declared.

1800

1950

ı4 Treaty of Paris.

35 Slavery was abolished Mauritius.

1867 A malaria epidemic killed half of the population.

The Dutch landing in Mauritius.

Bibliography

Addison, John; Hazareesingh, K: *A New History of Mauritius*, Rose Hill, 1993. Adone, Dany, *The acquisition of Mauritian Creole*, Philadelphia, 1994. Anderson, Charles: *Outlines of a plan submitted to Her Majesty's Government ...together with reasons for having recourse to India for the labourers who are required*, London, 1840. Anderson, Clare; Carter, Marina et al, *Forging the Rainbow*, Mauritius, 1997. Anville, Jean Baptiste Bourguignon: *Asia according to the Sieur d'Anville, divided into its empires, kingdoms and states, showing the European settlements in the East Indies and all the new discoveries made by the Russians, the Dutch and the English*, London, 1772. Archer, Edward Major: *A letter to the Right Honourable Lord John Russell, secretary of state for the Colonies : upon the policy of permitting emigration from the continent of India to the Mauritius*, London, 1840. Baker, Philip: *Isle de France creole: affinities and origins*, Karoma, 1982. Bengal Civilian: *Journal of Five Month's Residence in Mauritius*, Calcutta, 1838. Bernardin de Saint-Pierre, Jacques-Henri: *Voyage à l'Isle de France, à l'Île de Bourbon, au Cap de Bonne-Espérance, &c.*, Paris, 1773.– *Paul et Virginie*, Furne, 1856– Paul et Virginie, Paris. Backhouse, James: *A narrative of a visit to the Mauritius and South Africa*, London, 1844. Bory de Saint-Vincent, Jean : *Voyage dans les quatre principales îles des mers d'Afrique: fait par ordre du gouvernment, pendant les années neuf et dix de la République (1801 et 1802), avec l'histoire de la traversée du Capitaine Baudin jusqu'au Port-Louis de l'île Maurice. Collection de planches*, Paris, 1804. Baudelaire, Charles: *Les fleurs du mal et autres poèmes*, Tours, 1964. Bouton, Louis: *Plantes médicinales de Maurice*, Port Louis, 1864. Bradshaw, T: *Views in the Mauritius*, 1832. Bry, Johannus Theodorus de: *Indiæ Orientalis*, Frankfurt, 1601. Cantley, N: *Catalogue of Plants in the Royal Botanical Gardens*, Mauritius, 1880. Carter, Marina; Ng, James: *Colouring the Rainbow*, Mauritius, 1998. Charpentier de Cossigny, David, *Voyage à Canton*, Paris, 1799. Chazal, Malcy de: *The medicinal plants of Mauritius*, Berwickshire, 1989. Conrad, Joseph: *Twixt Land and Sea*, England,1982. Darwin, Charles: *The zoology of the voyage of HMS Beagle, under the command of Capt. Fitzroy, R.N., during 1832-36*, London, [1838]-40. Desvaux, Isabelle de Marigny; Valentin, Henriette Lagesse: *Living in Mauritius*, London, 1990. Durrell, Gerald: *Golden Bats and Pink Pigeon*, Fontana, 1987. Farquhar, R. T: *A Catalogue of the Exotic Plants cultivated in the Mauritius, at the Botanic Garden, Monplaisir, Reduit, and other places*, Mauritius, 1816. Freeman, J. J: *A Tour to South Africa with Notices of Natal, Mauritius, Madagascar, Ceylon, Egypt and Palestine*, London, 1851. Graham, Gerald S: *Great Britain in the Indian Ocean*, Oxford, 1967. Lee, Jacques K: *Sega, The Mauritian Folk Dance London*, 1990.– *Mauritius: Its Creole Language*, London, 1999. Le Guat, François: *A new voyage to the East-Indies by Francis Leguat and his companions, &c*, London, 1708. Ly-Tio-Fane, *Madeleine: Contacts between Schonbrunn and the Jardin du Roi at Isle de France (Mauritius) in the eighteenth century: an episode in the career of Nicolas Thomas Baudin*, Vienna, 1982. Milbert, Jacques G: *Voyagues pittoresques à l'Isle de France au Cap de Bonne Espérance et à Île Ténérife*, Paris, 1812. Mouat, Frederick John: *Rough Notes of a trip to Réunion, the Mauritius and Ceylon, &c*, Calcutta, 1852. North-Coombes, Alfred: *The vindication of François Leguat*, Port Louis, 1979. Olearius, Adam: *The Voyages & Travels of the Ambassadors sent by Frederick Duke of Holstein to the Great Duke of Muscovy, and the King of Persia*, London, 1662. Pitot, Édouard: *Arbres de l'île Maurice dessinés et lithographiés d'après Nature*, Port Louis, 1865. Prosper, Jean-Georges : *Indépendance et République*, 1996. — *Histoire de la littérature mauricienne de langue française*, EOI, 1978. — *L'île Maurice, au sommet de la vague économique francophone*, Paris, 1993. Rochon, Alexis: *Voyage à Madagascar et aux Indes orientales*, Paris, 1791. Staub, France: *Fauna of Mauritius and associated flora*, 1993. Teelock, Vijayalakshmi: *Teylandt Mauritius*, Rose Hill, 1998. Toussaint, Auguste: *Bibliography of Mauritius (1950-1954), covering the printed record, manuscripts, archivelia and cartographic material, &c*, Port Louis, 1956. Twain, Mark: *Following the Equator*, New York, 1989. Vaughan, Reginald: *The Mauritius herbarium, Mauritius*,1966. Vaux, Charles Grant, vicomte de: *The history of Mauritius*, London, 1801.

Topographical drawing of the Coin de Mire, 1804.

Coin de Mire, a small island off the north coast of Mauritius.

This edition of *Mauritius from its Origin* was published in August 201